For Ginny & Johnather

Love,

Robert Pitt

'99 NOV

F

KEEP EYE ON BALL,
IS MOST IMPORTANT
ONE THING I TELL YOU

Chris Widney *and* Richard Pitts

To Karen,
I'm so glad
you converted.
Chris '96

Richard Pitts 95

A FIRESIDE BOOK
Published by Simon & Schuster

NEW YORK   LONDON   TORONTO   SYDNEY   TOKYO   SINGAPORE

Fireside
Rockefeller Center
1230 Avenue of the Americas
New York, NY 10020

FIRESIDE and colophon are registered trademarks of Simon & Schuster Inc.

Designed by Stanley S. Drate/Folio Graphics Co., Inc.

Manufactured in the United States of America

10   9   8   7   6   5   4   3   2   1

Library of Congress Cataloging-in-Publication Data

Widney, Chris.
    Keep eye on ball, is most important one thing I tell you / Chris
Widney and Richard Pitts.
        p.   cm.
    "A Fireside book."
    1. Squash rackets (Game)   I. Pitts, Richard.   II. Title.
GV1004.W53   1996
796.34′3—dc20   95-44471
                  CIP

ISBN 0-684-81324-6

INTRODUCTION

In 1967, in Milwaukee, Wisconsin, Hashim Khan won his forty-fifth professional squash championship. In 1967, in downtown Manhattan, the artist Richard Pitts picked up his first squash racquet. Thus began a fascination that would last a lifetime.

What is it about the game of squash that is so intriguing? Perhaps it is the transformation that occurs whenever one sets foot in that strange, little room. Middle-aged businessmen suddenly become children. Introverts become tigers. Normally sane women are magically transformed into wild-eyed, ball-chasing fanatics. But why? What could possibly explain this bizarre metamorphosis?

"I–I don't know," answers Mr. Pitts, still dripping from a five-game match. "I love it. But I just don't know."

Who better to explain the mysteries of the game than the greatest player of all time? In his book, *The Khan Game,* generally regarded as the definitive squash text, Hashim Khan remembers his early days: "For a while I go to school, but it is like I am not there. I do not hear teacher, I do not see what he puts on blackboard. He thinks I am in his room, but I am in court, playing squash. I hear ball dash on wall, I see it bounce to me. I sit on floor in this school, yes, but my arm makes squash strokes!"

Granted, Mr. Khan may never have mastered the English language, but when faced with the endless angles, possibilities and mysteries of squash, no one has ever been more lucid.

Some say it began
in a men's prison . . .

Look in this court,
big box, walls every side, ceiling on top,
little door to go in and out.
In this court you see red stripes on floor and walls
to tell you where is out of bounds,
put foot in here to serve, such things.

Maybe to begin you buy low-price racquet, get good one later. In beginning, maybe you aim for ball, you hit wall. A few hits on that wall, goodbye that racquet.

Put out right hand
like you are to shake hands with this racquet.
If you see strings, turn racquet head.
You want to see wood only.

I do not think it is good idea,
woman playing squash with man opponent,
for reason she has handicap:
she is not so strong.

You go in court with
your opponent, he hits ball,
you hit ball, he hits ball.

This is idea of game.

Every time you see
opponent make ready for stroke,
you need quick answer for question,
"Where goes ball?"

Cat never takes eye from bird it tries to catch
and never you take eye away from ball you want to hit.
Keep eye on ball
is most important one thing I tell you.

Watch self!
Not rubber that racquet!

Not recommended for those with a heart condition

You run like crazy man round court
fifteen-twenty minutes,
you are all wet, saltwater in eyes,
chest jumping up and down to get air, legs weak.
You drop on floor. You all right?
Yes. Just not in shape.

Approximate energy expenditures:

ACTIVITY	CAL/HR
Basketball	564
Tennis	444
Dancing	420
Golf	348

SQUASH 924!

Many different ideas

how to get in shape for this game:

skip rope, lift weights, stretch exercises,

run on road, run upstairs-downstairs, run in one place

with feet coming off floor few inches.

Any way you do it,
it is important you get in shape.
How do you stroke properly,
move properly,
when all time you do not know
where you get next breath?

Stop Right There!

Did You Stretch?

First loose up your muscles before you play.
Do few sit-ups, some squats, touch toes, that is all.
Soon you are loose,
you can go in court.

I know one man, big, arm like blacksmith,
good condition, smart, fast on feet.
But you think he has fast ball?
Stiff, this man.
Too many tight muscles.

$\mathbb{S}$TROKES?
EASY:

The hip bone's connected to the backbone,

The backbone's connected to the shoulder bone,

The shoulder bone's connected to the wrist bone . . .

Forehand stroke: face right wall, feet wide apart maybe 3–4 inches more than shoulders. You unwind, arm and shoulder coming down, left shoulder starts coming up, forearm uncocks and moves flat at knee high, wrist uncocks and snaps, racquet hits ball a little in front of left knee, weight goes over to left leg, you follow through, and now you pick up right foot and take the big step where you want to go.

Backhand: you make like forehand
only you face left wall.

I say hit ball when it comes close to knee—
left knee for forehand stroke,
right knee for backhand stroke.
Do not change feet!

Do not make tense your body,
do not try too hard.
Swing like you are Tarzan of Apes on some vine.

I HEARD ABOUT THIS GREAT NEW SHOT . . .

Four shots only,
but possible to play such shots many different ways.
Like "robota," music instrument.
"Robota" has four strings only,
but how many sounds come from every string?
Same for squash racquets.

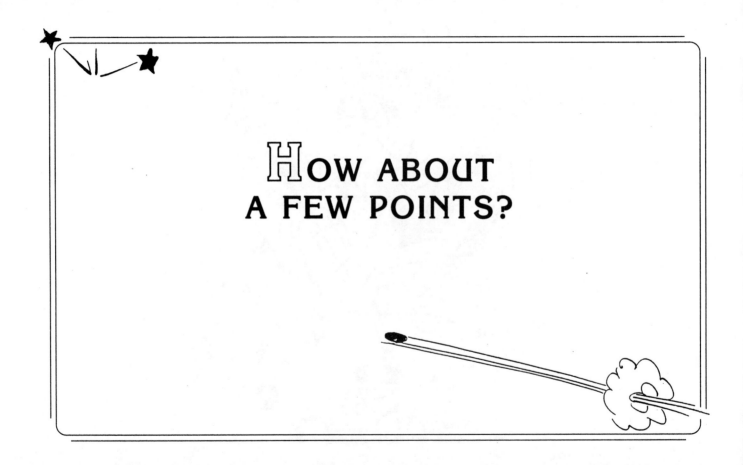

I make my stroke,
I move quick out of way
and all of a sudden that ball comes for me,
and I am hit.

LET? WHAT LET?

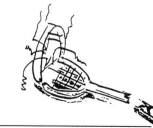

Somebody tells me squash player with good stroke makes ball go hundred miles in hour.

When you are in way of such ball, you never move self out in time.

*Rule 12. Interference**

12.1 When it is his turn to play the ball a player is entitled to freedom from interference from his opponent.

12.2 To avoid interference the opponent must make every effort to provide the player with:

  12.2.1 Unobstructed direct access to the ball.

  12.2.2 A fair view of the ball.

  12.2.3 Freedom to hit the ball.

  12.2.4 Freedom to play the ball directly to the front wall.

12.3 Interference occurs if the opponent fails to fulfill any of the requirements of rule 12.2, irrespective of whether he makes every effort to do so.

12.4 A player encountering what he considers to be interference has the choice of continuing play or of stopping and appealing to the referee.

  12.4.1 The correct method of appeal, whether a let or a stroke is sought by the player, is with the words, "Let please."

*The World Squash Federation.

When ball is coming close, and I start swing,
I put whole mind on that ball.
Nothing else I see.
One idea I have is to hit that ball,
and when I start stroke, I cannot stop.

Safety First. Hold up on your shot rather than risk injury to your opponent.*

*United States Squash Racquets Association Code of Conduct.

RACQUET UP

ELBOW IN   BEND THE WRIST

BEND THE KNEES   HOLD THE "T"   NO SHOTS

NOTHING CRAZY   KEEP IT DEEP

KEEP IT TIGHT   UP AND DOWN

HIT AND MOVE   HIT AND MOVE   GOOD WIDTH

GOOD LENGTH   GOOD DROPS   BE PATIENT

BE TOUGH   BE LOOSE   DON'T CHOKE

∘ ∘ ∘ 𝔸ND DON'T
FORGET
TO BREATHE.

You go in that court,
you have one idea: win game.
You do not worry about self.
You have game to win!

I speed up game. I make it go as fast as possible to end of point, win or lose.

If you are in way,
I am sorry, you are hit.

You send lob, lob, lob,
then you give cannonball serve straight back.
Opponent brain not believe his eye.
He sees ball, yes, he can do nothing in time.
Your point!

Maybe I make mistake, yes, of course.
Many times I hit tin, I miss that crack.
This is gamble, this is joy game.
When I start to have fear to make mistake,
then I think I am ready to stop this game.

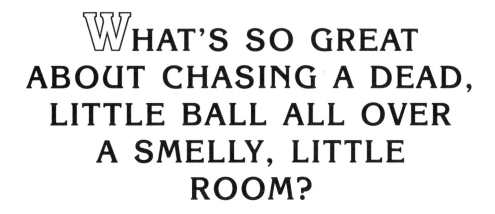

What's so great about chasing a dead, little ball all over a smelly, little room?

I have beginner student,
when he strokes ball right,
he says he feels like
Mickey Mantle hitting home run . . .
Mickey Mantle
is American baseball player.

Ball looks like it tries to leave game.
You aim front, it goes sideways.
It hits lights, ceiling, it flies in gallery.
You do *not* care.

You are in back, he sends ball up front.

You are in front, he sends it over head to back.

You are on right side, he sends it left.

That is all right,

you are happy in this court.

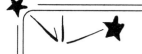

A GAME FOR A LIFETIME

A player with this many years
does not run like before.
But he gets experience,
he knows many things to do.
Experience is not as good as to be young—
there is nothing that good—
but anyway I give thanks for it.

How long can I play?
My uncle is eighty-seven
and he goes in squash court every day still.

I hope you have much joy in this game,
squash racquets!
Keep eye on ball . . .
is most important one thing I tell you.

Richard Pitts (artist) has been painting in New York City for over thirty years. His work has been exhibited at the David Findlay Gallery, New York City; Grace Borgenicht Gallery, New York City; Jacob's Ladder Gallery, Washington, D.C.; Ruthvin Gallery, Columbus, Ohio; as well as in major corporate and public collections. Although he holds the record for the most smashed squash racquets by any beginner, Mr. Pitts has risen to the "B" level in the metropolitan rankings.

Chris Widney (editor) has been playing and teaching squash in New York City for over ten years. When not on the squash court, Mr. Widney is an active playwright whose work has been produced Off-Broadway and around the country.

Hashim Khan (legend) is considered the greatest squash player and coach of all time. Originally from Peshawar, India (now Pakistan), he has played squash around the world and has won over fifty professional tournaments. Mr. Khan currently resides in Colorado where, in his seventies, he still plays competitive squash.